THE MAN FROM IRONBARK

The Man From Ironbark

Poem by
A. B. PATERSON

Illustrated by
QUENTIN HOLE

Collins
SYDNEY · LONDON

It was the man from Ironbark

who struck the Sydney town,

He wandered over street and park,

he wandered up

and down.

He loitered here, he loitered there, till he was like to drop,

Until at last in sheer despair he sought a barber's shop.

" 'Ere! shave my beard and whiskers off, I'll be a man of mark,
I'll go and do the Sydney toff up home in Ironbark."

The barber man was small and flash,
        as barbers mostly are,
He wore a strike-your-fancy sash,
        he smoked a huge cigar:

He was a humorist of note and keen at repartee,
He laid the odds and kept a "tote", whatever that may be.
And when he saw our friend arrive, he whispered "Here's a lark!
Just watch me catch him all alive this man from Ironbark."

There were some gilded youths that sat along the barber's wall,
Their eyes were dull, their heads were flat, they had no brains at all;
To them the barber passed the wink, his dexter eyelid shut,
"I'll make this bloomin' yokel think his bloomin' throat is cut."

And as he soaped and rubbed it in he made a rude remark:
"I s'pose the flats is pretty green up there in Ironbark."

A grunt was all reply he got; he shaved the bushman's chin,
Then made the water boiling hot and dipped the razor in.

He raised his hand, his brow grew black, he paused awhile to gloat,
Then slashed the red-hot razor-back across his victim's throat;
Upon the newly-shaven skin it made a livid mark—
No doubt it fairly took him in—the man from Ironbark.

He fetched a wild up-country yell might wake the dead to hear,
And though his throat, he knew full well, was cut from ear to ear,
He struggled gamely to his feet, and faced the murderous foe.

"You've done for me! you dog, I'm beat! one hit before I go!
I only wish I had a knife, you blessed murdering shark!
But you'll remember all your life the man from Ironbark."

He lifted up his hairy paw, with one tremendous clout
He landed on the barber's jaw, and knocked the barber out.

He set to work with tooth and nail, he made the place a wreck;
He grabbed the nearest gilded youth, and tried to break his neck.
And all the while his throat he held to save his vital spark,
And "Murder! Bloody Murder!" yelled the man from Ironbark.

A peeler man who heard the din came in to see the show;
He tried to run the bushman in, but he refused to go.

And when at last the barber spoke, and said " 'Twas all in fun—
'Twas just a little harmless joke, a trifle overdone."
"A joke!" he cried, "By George, that's fine; a lively sort of lark;
I'd like to catch that murdering swine some night in Ironbark."

And now while round the shearing-floor the listening shearers gape,
He tells the story o'er and o'er, and brags of his escape.
"Them barber chaps what keeps a tote, by George, I've had enough,
One tried to cut my bloomin' throat, but thank the Lord it's tough."

And whether he's believed or no, there's one thing to remark,
That flowing beards are all the go way up in Ironbark.

First published 1974 by William Collins (Australia) Ltd
Type set by Wallace & Knox Pty Ltd, Sydney
Printed by Dai Nippon Printing Co. (Hong Kong) Ltd